SOUTHERN STEAM IN COLOUR

Hugh Ballantyne

Copyright © Jane's Publishing Company Limited 1985

First published in the United Kingdom in 1985 by
Jane's Publishing Company Limited
238 City Road, London EC1V 2PU

ISBN 0 7106 0336 3

Printed in the United Kingdom
by Netherwood Dalton & Co Ltd

JANE'S

Cover illustrations

Front: The smoke beats down as rebuilt light Pacific No 34077
603 Squadron pounds down the West of England main line through
Brookwood with the 12.30 pm from Waterloo, the 'Bournemouth
Belle'. 17 October 1964. (*Hugh Ballantyne*)
Voigtlander CLR   50mm Skopar 2.8   Agfa CT18
f4, 1/500

Back: Quite dwarfed by its BR coaches, minute Stroudley 'Terrier'
A1X class No 32640 trundles across Langstone Bridge with the
3:35 pm train from Havant to Hayling Island. This bridge caused the
little 'Terriers' to survive as the branch motive power but also led to
closure of the line in November 1963 when its condition became unsafe
and the £400,000 then required to put it right could not be justified.
8 July 1962. (*Hugh Ballantyne*)
Voigtlander CLR   50mm Skopar 2.8   Perutz C18
f8, 1/250

Right: The famous landmark readily visible to travellers heading
across the Channel to England, the White Cliffs of Dover, tower 450 ft
above V class 'Schools' 4-4-0 No 30927 *Clifton* passing Shakespeare
Halt on an overcast summer Saturday morning with a train to Dover.
12 July 1958. (*T B Owen*)
Leica IIIc   85mm Sonnar   Kodachrome 8   f2.2, 1/200

Introduction

The Southern was the smallest of the four companies grouped in 1923 under the Railways Act of 1921 and its territory was clearly defined geographically in the south and west of England, extending from Broadstairs in East Kent to Padstow in Cornwall. Except in Devon and Cornwall there was very little penetration or competition by other railways, so it enjoyed firm control of services within most of its area. The Southern Railway was formed from three main companies, plus a few very small ones, which will be referred to in the text. Largest of the three was the London & South Western Railway (LSWR), which also controlled Southampton Docks; the South Eastern & Chatham Railway (SECR) served Kent and operated most of the Continental traffic, and was an earlier amalgamation of the London Chatham & Dover Railway (LCDR) and South Eastern Railway (SER); and finally came the compact but well run London Brighton & South Coast Railway (LBSCR). The headquarters of the Southern Railway was at Waterloo station in London, which was, and is, the largest station in the country.

I was a small boy living in Bath in the 1940s, when only a few Southern engines reached the city via the Somerset & Dorset Joint line. But on my first independent spotting journey down that railway to Templecombe in 1947, I was almost immediately awe-struck by the incredible sight to youthful eyes of an alien monster black machine charging into the station on an Exeter-bound express, bearing the mysterious number 21C9 and huge round nameplate with the strange words *Shaw Savill*. From that moment I became a great Southern admirer, and I hope you will derive pleasure from looking at this selection of Southern locomotives and trains, plus a few BR Standards, showing them as they used to be, going about their everyday business of earning their living.

Finally, I would like to extend sincere thanks to the photographers whose work is included in this book for their generosity in allowing the Publishers and myself the privilege of using their irreplaceable and unpublished original transparencies.

HUGH BALLANTYNE
Eccleshall, North Staffordshire
November 1984

Lovely old SER O1 class No 31048, one of 122 originally built by James Stirling as an O class in 1893 and rebuilt to the form seen here in 1908, shunting in Ashford shed yard. These engines performed yeoman service in Kent on lines with light axleloadings, but after nationalisation in 1948 many were quickly scrapped. This engine was one of the last four survivors and was withdrawn in October 1960. Fortunately No 31065 is preserved, although not on public display. August 1955. (*J M Jarvis*)
Kodak Retina   50mm Ektar 3.5   Kodachrome 8   f4, 1/100

A fine picture epitomising the Eastern Section of the Southern and the distinctive Maunsell 4-4-0s operated by the company. D1 class No 31735, from Bricklayers Arms shed, is seen passing Shortlands Junction on the SECR line with a Sunday afternoon van train from Ramsgate to Victoria, then a regular job for a 4-4-0. This engine was originally built as a D class to the design of Harry Wainwright by Sharp Stewart in 1901, and was rebuilt as D1 class to Maunsell's order by Beyer Peacock in 1921. Behind the train is the then new Shortlands Junction signal-box with the railway traction supply substation behind the first van. The second van is a bogie parcels miscellaneous van of the type built at Southern workshops between 1938 and 1953, of which there are still a few pre-war examples in service on the south eastern section. 7 June 1959. (*Rodney Lissenden*)
Agfa Silette   Agfa CT18

Above: A superb action picture of the third revolutionary Pacific designed by O V S Bulleid, 'Merchant Navy' class No 35003 *Royal Mail*, seen running hard on a down West of England express near Pirbright Junction, just west of Brookwood in Surrey. The evening sunlight clearly picks out the detail of this unrebuilt Pacific in its final form, the main points of interest being the cutaway cab for improved visibility and the casing removed between the buffer beam and cylinder. Note also the ribbing along the casing above the nameplate which was applied to the second batch of the class when thinner 'limpet' board plating was used to reduce the excessive weight of the original pair by over 3 tons. A regular performer from Exmouth Junction (Exeter) shed for many years, *Royal Mail* entered traffic in September 1941, was rebuilt in August 1959, and was included in the last group of Southern steam withdrawals in July 1967. 20 May 1958. (*T B Owen*)

Leica IIIc   85mm Sonnar
Kodachrome 8   f2.2, 1/200

Right: Another action picture, this time showing No 35003 *Royal Mail* in rebuilt form for comparison with the unrebuilt style of the engine shown above. Here *Royal Mail* is travelling fast at Fleet with the 1.30 pm Waterloo to Bournemouth express, under one of the lower quadrant signal gantries which were then such notable features on this section of the LSWR main line. 17 October 1964. (*Hugh Ballantyne*)

Voigtlander CLR   50mm 2.8 Skopar
Agfa CT18   f4, 1/500

Left: The SER was a compact system serving mainly East Sussex and Kent, but it did have one line which extended westwards through Surrey and into Berkshire, terminating at Reading. Today, the Reading–Redhill line remains a busy connecting route, but when this picture was taken Maunsell Moguls had command of most of the traffic. Here N class 2-6-0 No 31864 pulls out of Gomshall & Shere with the 9.45 am Reading to Redhill train one fine summer morning. 18 August 1962. (*Hugh Ballantyne*)
Voigtlander CLR   50mm 2.8 Skopar
Agfa CT18   f5.6, 1/250

Above: Between Guildford and Reigate the Reading–Redhill line traverses most attractive country as it runs parallel to and below the scarp of the heavily-wooded North Downs. The busiest intermediate station is at Deepdene, in Dorking, where Maunsell N class No 31870 is arriving with the 9.03 am (Sun) Reading to Redhill. 19 August 1962. (*Hugh Ballantyne*)
Voigtlander CLR   50mm 2.8 Skopar
Agfa CT18   f5.6, 1/250

7

Left: Even today the Isle of Wight system provides interest quite distinct from its parent system across the Solent. In the latter years of steam the Island railway was worked by small 0-6-0Ts of A1X and E1 classes, and at the end only by modified Adams 02 class 0-4-4Ts, all of which hauled rakes of vintage wooden-bodied compartment coaches with wide footboards. At Ryde the trains conveniently ran along the pier to Pier Head station adjacent to the steamer landing stage. In addition, there was a double track pier tramway, and in this fascinating picture the paddle steamer *Ryde* is alongside the pier as Class 02 No W35 *Freshwater* heads towards terra firma with a Ventnor train. The tramway, now closed, is clearly visible on the left. The *Ryde* was the second railway-owned vessel to carry this name and was built by William Denny & Bros at Dumbarton in 1937. She was the last paddle steamer constructed for service on the south coast and was quite small, being only 680 gross tons. She was withdrawn by BR in 1968 but still survives, and is now a floating marina anchored in the River Medina. 25 July 1964. (*R A Panting*)

Close up of an Island train at Ryde Esplanade station where 02 class No W35 *Freshwater* stands with the 1.18 pm Pier Head to Cowes train. The picture shows the attractive appearance of this small 0-4-4T class of which 60 were built by the LSWR to the design of William Adams between 1889 and 1895. Following the 1923 amalgamation, 20 of the class went over to the island prior to the second world war and a further three in 1947–49, so that eventually they became the only class in use. The island 02s were fitted with Westinghouse air brakes and the donkey pump can be seen attached to the near side of the smokebox. The other main feature was the enlarged coal bunker which increased coal capacity to 3 tons. All were named after places on the island and were given low running numbers in their own series. Unlike the rest of the BR loco fleet, the Isle of Wight engines had their front numbers painted on the buffer beam and an oval number plate affixed centrally to the rear of the bunker. 11 September 1965. (*Hugh Ballantyne*)

Voigtlander CLR   50mm 2.8 Skopar
Agfa CT18   f8, 1/60

Lined up outside Feltham shed are three of the five LSWR heavy tanks designed by Robert Urie, Nos 30516, 30520 and 30518, which were built at Eastleigh in 1921–22 and designated H16 class. These Pacific tanks followed Urie's earlier Class G16 4-8-0T hump shunters, and like the G16s were allocated to Feltham. How-ever, their duties were wider and they were primarily intended for interchange goods traffic in the London area. Sometimes they were press-ed into passenger service, particularly on Ascot race specials. During the sunset of their years in 1960 four of them went to Eastleigh to work Fawley branch oil trains for a year or so, before returning to Feltham and eventual withdrawal at the end of 1962. 2 December 1962. (*G W Morrison*)

Zeiss Contaflex   Tessar   Agfa CT18 f2.8

As seen in the picture opposite, the bulk of the ferro-concrete Feltham shed building is prominent behind the locomotive; it is a sobering thought that this building and all the massive SR marshalling yard has now completely vanished. This picture shows No 31893, one of Maunsell's three-cylinder 6 ft coupled U1 class 2-6-0s of which there were 21, including the prototype which was rebuilt from K1 class 2-6-4T No A890. This engine was built at Eastleigh in 1931 and spent some years at Fratton shed, Portsmouth. After the war all the class was concentrated on the SECR lines for Kent Coast trains until electrification in June 1959, when again they moved and No 31893 went to Feltham. The last of the class was withdrawn in July 1963. 17 October 1959. (*Rodney Lissenden*)
Agfa Silette   Agfa CT18

Left: Rebuilt 'Battle of Britain' class No 34088 *213 Squadron*, pride of Stewarts Lane shed, carrying the full 'Golden Arrow' regalia and turned out in the impeccable condition for which 'the Lane' was justly famous, pounds up the 1 in 100 rise from Beckenham Junction to Shortlands on the old LCDR route, heading south-eastwards non-stop to Dover Marine with one of the Southern's top trains, the 10.00 am 'Golden Arrow' from Victoria. 17 September 1960. (*Rodney Lissenden*)
Agfa Silette   Agfa CT18

Above: The returning all-Pullman 'Golden Arrow', 6.13 pm from Dover Marine to Victoria, seen this time with spotless unrebuilt 'Battle of Britain' class No 34085 *501 Squadron* at its head, threading its way out of Dover past the loco shed (just out of the picture to the right) before getting into its stride for the 1 hour 37 minute dash up to Victoria, 78 miles away. 23 May 1959. (*T B Owen*)
Leica IIIc   85mm Sonnar
Kodachrome 8   f2.4, 1/100

Left: Because of soaring costs and delays in obtaining replacement boilers for the ageing fleet of Class B4 dock shunters at Southampton, Bulleid was forced by 1945 to consider suitable replacements. At the time there were many surplus British and American WD six-coupled tanks for sale. The British locos had an 11 ft wheelbase against the 10 ft of the Americans, and the latter were in generally better mechanical condition, so after testing WD No 4326 (later BR No 30074) the SR bought it and 13 more (plus one extra for spares) for £2500 each in 1947. They gave good service at Southampton

Docks until diesels arrived in 1962. Some then went into departmental service, but No 30072 went to Guildford in March 1963 as replacement shed pilot to B4 No 30089 (see page 50), were it is seen five months later performing everyday chores, which continued until the end of steam on the Southern in July 1967. This engine is now actively employed on the Keighley & Worth Valley Railway in Yorkshire. 11 August 1963. (*Hugh Ballantyne*)
Voigtlander CLR   50mm 2.8 Skopar
Agfa CT18   f8, 1/60

Below: A general view of the half roundhouse at Guildford one busy morning. USA class 0-6-0T No 30072 is prominent on shed pilot duties whilst Q1 class 0-6-0 No 33032 is being turned before coming off shed. Inside can be seen more locos including Maunsell Moguls and another Q1. Finally, on the left, one of the now vanished 1937-built Southern electric 4-COR units is emerging from the tunnel with a Portsmouth to Waterloo train. This shed was closed in July 1967; all its facilities have now been completely swept away and the site is a car park. 11 August 1963. (*Hugh Ballantyne*)
Voigtlander CLR   50mm 2.8 Skopar
Agfa CT18   f8, 1/60

Above: Immediately to the east of Honiton a narrow ridge of hills rising in places to 800 feet above sea level caused the LSWR main line to climb sharply and tunnel under the ridge to a summit just west of that tunnel. Here rebuilt 'West Country' class No 34032 *Camelford* is coming steadily up the 1 in 80 gradient through the lovely green landscape of south east Devon with the 11.45 am Waterloo to Ilfracombe train on a hot summer afternoon. No doubt the passengers were keenly looking forward to arriving at the North Devon seaside resort for their holidays. 27 June 1984. (*Hugh Ballantyne*)

Voigtlander CLR   50mm 2.8 Skopar
Agfa CT18   f4, 1/500

Right: Just a few miles east of the location opposite, near the start of the westbound climb to Honiton Tunnel, was the rural station of Seaton Junction. Its purpose was simply as a changing point for the 4¼ mile branch running due south to the small seaside resort of Seaton, served by a frequent shuttle service from the junction. In the orderly way of Southern Railway operating, an up local hauled by 'Battle of Britain' class No 34051 *Winston Churchill* is standing at the up platform, and the tall LSWR bracket up starter shows the train has a clear road. The timetabling on this line was based on regular-interval fast through trains backed up by all stations locals which dovetailed into the main stops, so providing the public with an excellent service between what are now regarded as inter-city stations and a network of local stations. After control of the line passed to the WR all this was swept away, with both branch line and junction closed. 18 August 1964. (*Hugh Ballantyne*)

Voigtlander CLR   50mm 2.8 Skopar
Agfa CT18   f5.6–8, 1/125

Above: A scene at Dorchester South showing the old terminus station of the line from Southampton. This was situated at right angles to the GWR line to Weymouth, designed with the intention of the LSWR route continuing towards Exeter. This never materialised, and when the sharp curve linking the two lines was opened in 1857 a new down platform was provided for Southampton–Weymouth trains. No corresponding up platform was built, which meant all up trains had the inconvenience of backing into the original terminus platform. This anachronism lasted until 1970 when a new up platform was constructed and the old station closed. Here 'West Country' class No 34107 *Blandford* stands at the old terminus station with the 1.30 pm Weymouth to Waterloo express. No 34107 was renamed, correctly, *Blandford Forum* in October 1952. 24 April 1952. (*T B Owen*)
Leica IIIc 50mm Summitar
Kodachrome 8 f3.5, 1/60

Right: One of Maunsell's later series of 'King Arthurs', N15 class No 30805 *Sir Constantine*, in the evening of its days sweeping down the 1 in 52 gradient out of Bincombe Tunnel on the last stages of the journey to Weymouth with a train from Bournemouth. This engine had been displaced from the Eastern Section two months earlier by the Kent Coast electrification and finished its days on the Western Section working from Eastleigh. No 30805 was the penultimate 'Arthur' to be built, being completed at Eastleigh in 1927, and was withdrawn in November 1959. 4 July 1959. (*T B Owen*)
Leica IIIc 85mm Sonnar
Kodachrome 8 f2.8, 1/200

In North Kent the SER had a short branch off the Port Victoria line to the small resort at Allhallows-on-Sea situated on the Kentish side of the Thames estuary and facing across to the much better known holiday town of Southend-on-Sea. The area is flat and rather windswept, as evidenced by the weather-beaten condition of the terminus station, where two SECR Wainwright H class 0-4-4Ts Nos 31570 and 31531 stand each side of the island platform with trains to Gravesend Central. The branch service was withdrawn in 1961 and the station closed, although the section as far as Grain remains open for oil traffic. August 1959. (*D A Soggee*)

Agfa Silette   Kodachrome 8   f3.5, 1/125

An Allhallows branch train comprising one of the 66 Wainwright H class 0-4-4Ts, No 31518, which was built at Ashford in 1909, with two non-corridor coaches in early BR red livery, standing at Gravesend Central station. On the right a 4-EPB unit No S5199, in Southern green, is working a Maidstone West–Charing Cross service. August 1960. (*D A Soggee*)

Agfa Silette   *Kodachrome 8*   *f3.5, 1/125*

Top: Portrait of a magnificent Brighton Atlantic No 32424 *Beachy Head* on its home territory at Brighton shed. The LBSCR had some elegant locomotives and Douglas Earle Marsh, who became CME in 1904, coming from the Great Northern Railway, fully appreciated the usefulness of the large-boiler Atlantic type. His first batch of five was built by Kitson and classified H1. A second series of six Atlantics, classified H2, with larger cylinders and straight running plates, was ordered in 1911 and they entered traffic late that year and early in 1912. This engine, H2 class No 32424, was built at Brighton Works in 1911 and was the last Atlantic tender engine to remain in service in Great Britain. This picture shows it after the last run which had been on an RCTS special from Victoria to Newhaven, then finally proceeding light engine to Brighton. On that last journey with a 255 ton load *Beachy Head* managed a very creditable 70 mph at Balcombe. 13 April 1958. (*T B Owen*)
Leica IIIc   50mm Summitar
Kodachrome 8   f4.2, 1/60

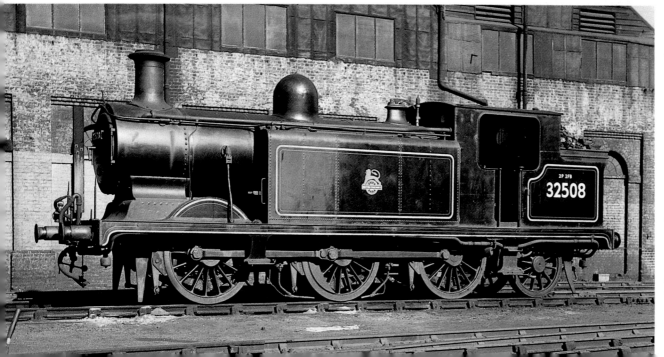

Left: The lower picture shows one of R J Billinton's E4 class 0-6-2Ts No 32508, which were known as 'Large Radials'. These were useful engines working on both goods and passenger duties and became a large class comprising 75 locomotives. This one was built at Brighton in 1900 as No 508 *Bognor* and eventually withdrawn in the livery shown above by the Southern Region in 1960. One, as LBSCR No 473 *Birchgrove*, is preserved on the Bluebell Railway. 13 April 1958. (*T B Owen*)
Leica IIIc   50mm Summitar
Kodachrome 8   f4, 1/60

This is one of 50 diminutive Stroudley-designed A1X class 0-6-0T known as 'Terriers', built as No 35 *Morden* in 1878, later becoming Southern No 2635. In August 1946 it became Brighton Works shunter and was renumbered in service stock as 377S. Following the repainting of sister engine *Boxhill* in the splendid Stroudley yellow livery, the works had the excellent idea of applying the same livery to No 377S, and in 1947 it emerged so painted, adorned with a copper chimney cap and lettered *Brighton Works*, where it is seen in this picture. Renumbered by BR as DS377, the locomotive stayed until the works closed in 1959 and returned to general stock as No 32635, finally being withdrawn in March 1963. 13 April 1958. (*T B Owen*)
Leica IIIc   85mm Sonnar
Kodachrome 8   f4.5, 1/60

23

I think this picture helps portray the Maunsell V class 'Schools' 4-4-0 as a leading contender for the title of most elegant locomotive type ever built. Here is No 30926 *Repton* just having received the royal treatment at 'the Lane'. Stewarts Lane shed in London was justly famous for the standard to which it always turned out its locomotives, especially those working Royal Train duties. *Repton* was the last 'Schools' to receive general repairs, at Ashford Works in October 1960, and here it is 19 months later ready to haul the Royal Train from Victoria to Tattenham Corner on Derby Day. Note the special burnished front hook and coupling which Stewarts Lane kept for such occasions. This engine was withdrawn in December 1962 and has been preserved, albeit on the 'wrong' side of the Atlantic. It languishes little used at Steamtown, Vermont, but perhaps one day may return to its native England – as a live stable mate for sister No 928 resplendent on the Bluebell Railway? 31 May 1962. *(Rodney Lissenden)* *Agfa Silette   Agfa CT18*

Although not taken at Stewarts Lane, nor seen in the pristine condition in which this locomotive was kept when at that shed, 'Britannia' class 7 No 70004 *William Shakespeare* was a famous Stewarts Lane resident from shortly after construction in 1951 to its transfer away from the Southern. Following building at Crewe, it received an exhibition finish for display at the South Bank, London, during the Festival of Britain, after which in October 1951 it started its working life on the Southern Region. It disgraced itself almost immediately, suffering a fractured side rod whilst travelling at speed near Headcorn working the up 'Golden Arrow', but quickly returned to traffic and shared this prestigious duty and other Continental Boat Train workings with No 70014 *Iron Duke*. Here No 70004 is seen much later on when, thanks to the cooperation of BR, it was brought from Stockport Edgeley shed back to the Southern to work an LCGB special train, the 'A2 Commemorative Tour'! Commendably clean for the time, although bereft of nameplates and full lining, this fine engine still makes a pleasing sight standing outside Salisbury shed. 14 August 1966. (*Hugh Ballantyne*)
Voigtlander CLR   50mm 2.8 Skopar
Agfa CT18   f8–11, 1/60

25

Above: A 'Battle of Britain' class Pacific leaving Padstow, the most westerly point of the Southern Railway. No 34078 *222 Squadron* is crossing the bridge over a tributary of the River Camel just south of the town at the start of its long journey through rural North Cornwall and Devon to Exeter, a distance of 88 miles, with the 8.30 am train from Padstow. 25 July 1964. (*T B Owen*)

Leica M2   50mm Summicron
Kodachrome II   f3.2, 1/250

No 34078 *222 Squadron* again seen at work on the North Cornwall line arriving at Camelford station with the 11.00 am Padstow to Waterloo train. The station was situated over a mile from

this remote little Cornish market town and this long western extension of the former LSWR was aptly described as 'the withered arm' by railway historian T W Roche. Virtually all the Southern lines in Cornwall have now disappeared, this section from Meldon Junction to Wadebridge closing on 3 October 1966. 4 July 1964. (*Peter A Fry*)

Kodak Retinette 1B   Agfa CT18

Newhaven Harbour was controlled by an independent company but worked in close cooperation with the LBSCR and its successor, and the use of Stroudley 0-6-0T 'Terriers' for shunting and light work at Newhaven was standard practice for over 75 years. Indeed *Fenchurch* was sold to the Harbour company in 1898. One of the jobs these little engines were required to do was to shunt the West Quay branch to Newhaven west breakwater. This picture shows the last train to perform this duty with No 32678 propelling its train towards the breakwater situated below the distinctive chalk cliffs on the west side of this channel port. No 32678 was built as No 78 *Knowle* in 1880, was withdrawn by BR in 1963 and sold to Sir Billy Butlin of holiday camp fame. After a stint on display at his Minehead camp, this engine is now resident on the West Somerset Railway. 30 July 1963. (*T B Owen*)
Leica M2   50mm Summicron
Kodachrome II   f3.2, 1/250

The 4½ mile branch from Havant to Hayling Island in Hampshire was severely restricted due to the weight limit imposed on Langstone Bridge (see rear cover), so 'Terriers' held sway exclusively as the branch motive power. Here on a busy summer Saturday No 32650 hurries across the A3023 main road leading to the island, watched over by the crossing keeper who in the very few spare moments between the frequent shuttle train service obviously tends his adjacent well kept cabbage patch. No 32650 was built at Brighton in 1876 as No 50 *Whitechapel* and was withdrawn in November 1963, following closure of the Hayling Island branch to all traffic on 4 November. It was sold for preservation to the Borough of Sutton & Cheam in 1964 and is now in regular service on the Kent & East Sussex Railway as No 10 *Sutton*. 8 July 1962. (*Hugh Ballantyne*)

Voigtlander CLR   50mm 2.8 Skopar
Agfa CT18   f5.6, 1/250

During the 1930s the Southern directed its energies and financial resources mainly towards extending electrification; steam locomotives tended to be ordered as replacements of older engines or for essential maintenance of the services provided. This picture shows Q class 0-6-0 No 30531, one of 20 built in 1938–39 as replacement engines for secondary goods and passenger work, and which proved to be Maunsell's last design. Their appearance, somewhat dated by the late-1930s, as a traditional simple British 0-6-0 type of workhorse, was pure Maunsell, and when treated moderately were reliable engines. This one, seen at Eastleigh, was fitted by Bulleid with a Lemaitre blastpipe and large diameter chimney. It was withdrawn in 1964 but sister engine No 30541 is restored and working on the Bluebell Railway. 10 June 1961. (G W Morrison)

Contaflex   2.8 Tessar   Agfa CT18

Top: Maunsell's best known express passenger engine was the handsome four-cylinder 'Lord Nelson' class 4-6-0. The prototype No 850 *Lord Nelson* was completed at Eastleigh in 1926 and 15 more followed in 1928–29. Numerous experiments were carried out to individual members of the class whilst in service and this picture shows No 30856 *Lord St Vincent* in final form just ex-works from Eastleigh, fitted with Lemaitre blastpipe and large chimney, and painted in the attractive BR lined green livery. *Lord St Vincent* was scrapped in September 1962, but fortunately the prototype survives and performs regularly on approved BR steam lines. 18 September 1960. (*Rodney Lissenden*)
Agfa Silette   Agfa CT18

Right: In 1913 L B Billinton introduced to the LBSCR five powerful 2-6-0s of attractive and well-proportioned design for heavy goods work. They proved a godsend to the Running Department during the First World War hauling troop specials and 1000 ton trains on the main line. Five more were built during the war, followed by a final batch of seven in 1920–21. The K class spent most of their working lives on the Central Section but some repairs were effected at Eastleigh, the location of this ex-works No 32341 resplendent in BR lined black livery. Although these engines gave reliable service, all 17 were suddenly withdrawn towards the end of the 1962 in what was stated to be an accounting exercise to maintain the SR's withdrawal programme! This seemed nothing less than a disgraceful way in which to waste the assets of a business, sadly a familiar tale with BR at the time. 18 September 1960. (*Rodney Lissenden*)
Agfa Silette   Agfa CT18

This portrait can be compared with the 'Schools' on page 24 as it shows No 30921 *Shrewsbury* in BR lined black livery and one of 20, exactly half the class, which Bulleid subsequently fitted with a Lemaitre blastpipe and wide chimney. This was despite the fact there had never been any serious complaints of poor steaming or erratic performance. No 30921 is seen at St Leonards shed, Hastings, a well known stamping ground for the 'Schools' used on the restricted loading gauge line to Tonbridge, and over which they performed superbly on Charing Cross services until dieselisation in 1957. This engine was built in 1933 and was included with the last batch of class withdrawals in December 1962. 15 May 1954. (*T B Owen*)
Leica IIIc   50mm Summitar
Kodachrome 8   f3.2, 1/100

The Kent Coast lines also saw a great deal of 'Schools' activity and Ramsgate shed invariably had 10 or more allocated there. Electric services to London via the LCDR line commenced in 1959 and so the shed was reduced in status to a stabling point for the few remaining steam workings in the area. Here No 30925 *Cheltenham*, in lined black livery, waits to leave with the 5.45 pm to Charing Cross via Dover and the SER main line. Fortunately this engine is preserved as part of the national collection, but since withdrawal by BR in 1962 has regrettably only been seen active during 1980, after appearing earlier at Rainhill 150 and Dinting. 14 June 1959. *(Rodney Lissenden)*
Agfa Silette   Agfa CT18

Left: The Salisbury–Exeter main line, then double track throughout, is a real switchback and called for engine working of the highest order. About this time the 'Atlantic Coast Express', with its 60 mph running for the 75.8 miles each way between Salisbury and Sidmouth Junction, was probably the hardest steam passenger duty in the country. Four months before dieselisation, No 35016 *Elders Fyffes* surges westbound up the rise beyond Wilton with the down train, 11.00 am from Waterloo. 18 April 1964. (*Hugh Ballantyne*) *Voigtlander CLR 50mm 2.8 Skopar Agfa CT18   f2.8, 1/500*

Right: On a cold winter's day a well cleaned rebuilt 'Battle of Britain' class No 34052 *Lord Downing* leaves Salisbury with the 10.10 am (Sun) cross-country train from Plymouth to Portsmouth. 8 March 1964. (*Hugh Ballantyne*) *Voigtlander CLR 50mm 2.8 Skopar Agfa CT18 f4–5.6, 1/250*

Left: At Holes Bay Junction, Poole, where the line from Blandford and Wimborne meets the main line from Dorchester coming across the causeway, 'Merchant Navy' class No 35017 *Belgian Marine* swings over the points with a Weymouth to Waterloo train. This was a Weymouth-based engine, built in 1945, rebuilt 1957 and withdrawn in August 1965, three months after the picture was taken. The photograph well portrays the area around Poole Harbour, regarded as the finest natural harbour in England and a noted nature reserve, much of which is bordered by heath and woodland. Holes Bay forms a shallow lagoon to the north of the main part of the Harbour. 29 May 1965. (*Alan Trickett*)
Zeiss Contina
Agfa CT18   f4, 1/500

Right: In an attractive setting east of Parkstone station 'Battle of Britain' No 34064 *Fighter Command* nears the top of the sharp 1 in 60 climb from sea level at Poole up to Branksome before levelling off and coasting to the principal intermediate stop at Bournemouth Central with the 11.17 am Weymouth to Waterloo train. The picture clearly shows the Giesl oblong ejector which was fitted to this engine (the only one so equipped) in May 1962. No 34064 was built at Brighton in 1947 and withdrawn in May 1966. 17 July 1965. (*Alan Trickett*)
Zeiss Contina
Agfa CT18   f4, 1/500

Left: For obvious geographical reasons the Isle of Wight network had to be very self-contained, and locomotive and carriage workshop facilities were provided at Ryde St Johns. All work except heavy boiler repairs were carried out at Ryde and the standard of finish can be gauged by this picture of the vintage LBSCR non-corridor coach just repainted in green livery. 02 class 0-4-4T No W27 *Merstone* stands under the hoist receiving attention and minus one pair of driving wheels. 4 August 1965.
(*D Trevor Rowe*)

Above: Another view at Ryde St Johns looking north towards the station showing 02 class No W14 *Fishbourne* pulling away from a stop, with the 12.18 pm Ryde Pier to Cowes train. On the right No W16 *Ventnor* is visible under the hoist. By this date the Island system was reduced to just the two lines from Ryde to Ventnor and Cowes. St Johns was the location of the last remaining loco shed, which was situated behind the signalbox adjacent to the west side of the station. 11 September 1965. (*Hugh Ballantyne*)
Voigtlander CLR   50mm 2.8 Skopar
Agfa CT18   f5.6–8, 1/125

39

Left: M7 class 0-4-4T
No 30129 makes a fine sight
in the early morning sunlight
just accelerating after
coming over the points at
Lymington Junction with
the 7.35 am train from
Lymington Pier to
Brockenhurst. The junction
layout behind the engine can
be clearly seen, with the
Lymington branch going to
the left, main line to
Bournemouth straight on,
and the original route from
Southampton to Dorchester,
which was known as
'Castleman's Corkscrew'
after its promoter, turning to
the right. 27 July 1963.
(T B Owen)
Leica M2
50mm Summicron
Kodachrome II
f2.8, 1/250

Right: M7 class No 30052
near Boldre Bridge hauling a
train from Lymington Pier
to Brockenhurst. By the time
this picture was taken only
nine remained in service of
the 105 built and this engine
was one of the seven
survivors at Bournemouth
retained there to work this
branch and the Swanage
line. In May 1964 they were
all withdrawn and so ended
the era of push-and-pull
operation on the Southern
Region, but the branch
continued to be worked by
Ivatt 2-6-2Ts and BR
Standard 2-6-4Ts until 2
April 1967 and was the last
steam-operated branch line
in the country. It was
subsequently electrified and
remains open for passenger
traffic. 26 April 1964. *(Alan Trickett)*
Zeiss Contina   Agfa CT18

Above: A scene at Reading Southern station showing a section of railway which has completely disappeared. This station was the terminus of the long SER line from Redhill which extended westwards through Surrey and into Berkshire. Although this important link route via Guildford remains active, all trains now run over the connection on to the former GWR line and Southern Region trains use a new platform at what was previously called Reading General. The adjacent Southern station was closed in September 1965 and the spot where Maunsell U class No 31639 waits to leave with a train to Redhill is now a car park. In the distance the former SER locomotive shed can also be seen. 24 October 1964. (*Hugh Ballantyne*)
Voigtlander CLR   50mm 2.8 Skopar Agfa CT18   f8, 1/60

Right: On a sunny autumn afternoon one of the 80 Maunsell N class Moguls No 31410 gallops across the Cove Brook bridge between Blackwater and Farnborough North with the 2.50 pm Reading to Redhill train. These very useful engines worked a variety of goods, semi-fast and excursion trains all over the Southern system. This locomotive was one of the last batch of 15 which were built at Brighton in 1933 and it was withdrawn from Guildford shed in November 1964. 17 October 1964. (*Hugh Ballantyne*)
Voigtlander CLR   50mm 2.8 Skopar Agfa CT18   f4, 1/500

The 0-6-0 C class goods engines built by Wainwright for the SECR were elegant, robust and functional, but owed something in their design to William Kirtley, the Loco Superintendent of the LCDR. One hundred and nine were built between 1900 and 1906, 79 by the company at Ashford and Longhedge, and 30 by contractors Neilson Reid and Sharp Stewart; all but two passed into BR ownership on 1 January 1948. This fine vintage picture shows No 31723 hauling a lovely old SECR 'Birdcage' set of coaches working the 9.45 am Reading to Guildford local train near North Camp. 2 March 1957. (*T B Owen*)

Leica IIIc   85mm Sonnar
Kodachrome 8   f2.3, 1/200

Passengers waiting at Shepherd's Well, on the main line of the LCDR, for their local train to Dover watch C class 0-6-0 No 31481 bring a goods into the station. This was the junction for the erstwhile Colonel Stephens owned East Kent Railway, a remnant of which still serves the small coalfield in this area. No 31481 was built at the Longhedge, London, works of the SECR in 1904. One member of the class survives, restored in the full glory of the Wainwright SECR livery as No 592 and today provides a splendid sight on the Bluebell Railway. 23 March 1959. (T B Owen)

Leica IIIc   50mm Summitar
Kodachrome 8   f2.8, 1/200

Left: The motor coaches in the coach park at Ryde look almost as dated as this typical Isle of Wight train of the 1960s with 02 class 0-4-0T No W14 *Fishbourne* leaving Ryde Esplanade with the 1.20 pm Pier Head to Shanklin train. 22 August 1964. *(Hugh Ballantyne)*
Voigtlander CLR   50mm 2.8 Skopar
Agfa CT18   f5.6, 1/250

Above: A view of Ventnor station, located 276 feet above sea level in this pleasant seaside town on the south side of the island. Once the town boasted two stations, but the branch from Merstone to Ventnor West was closed in 1952. This station remained the terminus of the 'main line' on the island until the end of 1966 when steam services were withdrawn pending electrification. However, the section from Shanklin to Ventnor, with its 1312 yard tunnel through the 787 foot

high mass of St Boniface Down, partly seen in the top left of the picture, was not reopened. This picture shows No W33 *Bembridge* taking water having just come off the 1.25 pm train from Ryde Pier Head, after which it will run round and take the train back to Ryde. 11 September 1965. *(Hugh Ballantyne)*
Voigtlander CLR   50mm 2.8 Skopar
Agfa CT18   f5.6–8, 1/60

Left: A portrait of 'Battle of Britain' class No 34051 *Winston Churchill*, seen in the final form of the unrebuilt Bulleid light Pacifics, taken at Bournemouth shed. This engine had the sombre task of working the funeral train of its namesake, our great wartime hero and statesman, from Waterloo to Handborough in Oxfordshire on 30 January 1965. No 34051 was immaculately turned out and when seen hauling the funeral train of five Pullman cars and a PMV van, the latter repainted umber and cream for the occasion, it was a credit both to the Nine Elms loco staff who had prepared the engine and the Southern Region as a whole. No 34051 was withdrawn in September 1965 and is preserved in the national collection, although it has not been steamed. 2 May 1965. (*Alan Wild*)
Kodak Retinette 1A   Perutz C18

Below: A view of Bournemouth shed, looking westwards from the signalbox located above the platform roof, showing its cramped position at the west end of Central station. In contrast to the grimy Pacifics on shed, 'Battle of Britain' No 34082 *615 Squadron* in the foreground makes a pleasing spectacle as it runs into the station with an up train to Waterloo. Bournemouth shed survived until the end of steam on the Southern in July 1967 but now has completely disappeared with construction of an inner relief road bridge over the site, which now forms a car park. 15 November 1964. (*Alan Trickett*)
Zeiss Contina   Agfa CT18

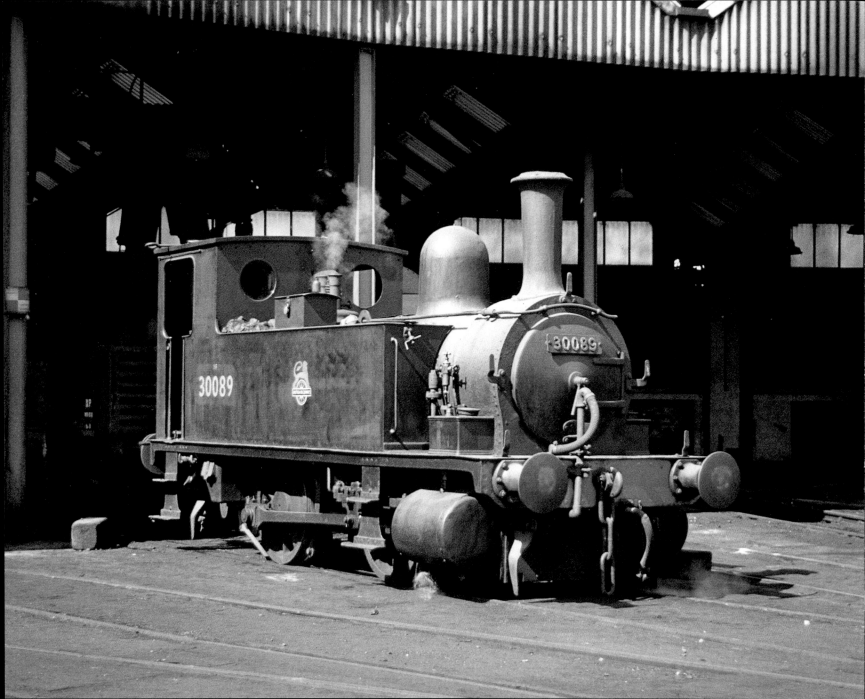

Left: No 30089, one of 25 small 0-4-0T dock shunters built for the LSWR to the design of William Adams and known as Class B4, simmers gently outside its abode at Guildford, where it was employed as shed pilot between 1957 and its demise in March 1963. Previously No 30089 had spent, with others of the class, many years in the docks at Southampton and in keeping with dock company tradition of naming engines was given the name *Trouville* during its time there. 15 June 1959.
(Peter W Gray)
Agfa Super Silette
Kodachrome I

Right: Another longstanding B4 class survivor was No 30102, which in company with sister No 30096 shared the shunting duties at Winchester in the latter days of their existence. No 30102, named *Granville* whilst at Southampton Docks, was withdrawn in September 1963 and is seen here shunting at the goods shed near the end of its BR working life. Fortunately it was bought in 1964 by Sir Billy Butlin, who promptly despatched it north of the border for display at his Ayr Holiday Camp. It was subsequently sent to Bressingham Gardens, near Diss in Norfolk, where it can be seen today. Circa 1963.
(Basil Roberts)
Kodak Retinette 1B
Agfa CT18

THE ONLY ENGINES PERMITTED TO PASS THIS BOARD ARE THE CLASS 2, B4 & 204 H.P. DIESEL.

Left: One of the 5 ft 6 in coupled Maunsell Moguls, N class No 31846, on a typical duty in the extreme west of the Southern network, pulls away from Wadebridge and heads alongside the River Camel with the 1.00 pm train from Padstow to Exeter Central. Traversing attractive but sparsely populated countryside in Cornwall and Devon, this train will take 3 hours 13 minutes to complete its 88 mile journey. 4 July 1964. (*Peter A Fry*)
Kodak Retinette 1B
Agfa CT18

Right: An interesting station scene at Bodmin North where 02 class 0-4-4T No 30236 has just arrived with a train from Wadebridge. The railway between Bodmin North and Wadebridge formed part of the Bodmin & Wadebridge Railway which opened in July 1834 as an isolated line and was one of the earliest railways in the country. Although acquired by the LSWR in 1847 it was not connected to the parent system until 1895. In 1964 the through service between the two towns was withdrawn, and this historic station was closed when the last shuttle railcar service ran from Boscarne Junction on 28 January 1967. 2 May 1959. (*D A Soggee*)
Agfa Silette
Kodachrome 8
f3.5, 1/125

Right: Deep in the New Forest a Maunsell Mogul heads for Brockenhurst with the 12.47 pm Saturdays train from Southampton Terminus to Wimborne. This engine, U class No 31619, was built at Brighton in 1928 and was originally to have been in a batch of 2-6-4Ts in which it had been allocated the name *River Taw*. However, following the adverse publicity created by the unfortunate derailment of 2-6-4T No A800 *River Cray* at Sevenoaks in 1927, orders were immediately given for this group of engines to be constructed as 2-6-0s and the names omitted. 9 June 1962. *(Alan Wild)*
Kodak Retinette 1A
Perutz C18   f4, 1/250

Opposite: Rebuilt light Pacific No 34090 *Sir Eustace Missenden Southern Railway* going well past Lymington Junction signalbox on the short sharp 1 in 103 rise towards Sway with the 10.30 am Waterloo to Weymouth. 27 July 1963. *(T B Owen)*
Leica M2
50mm Summicron
Kodachrome II
f2.5, 1/500

Inset: The distinctive commemorative nameplate attached to rebuilt light Pacific No 34090 which was named on 15 February 1949 at Waterloo as a tribute to the former General Manager of the Southern Railway. 24 June 1964. *(Hugh Ballantyne)*
Voigtlander CLR
50mm 2.8 Skopar
Agfa CT18   f5.6, 1/30

It is fair to say that all three constituent companies amalgamated into the SR in January 1923 had many elegant locomotives and that their four-coupled engines were particularly pleasing to the eye. From the largest of the three companies, the LSWR, perhaps the most famous type was Dugald Drummond's lovely T9 class 4-4-0. Sixty-six of these locomotives were built between 1899 and 1901. This fine action picture shows No 30724, built by Dubs & Co in 1899, on a bright winter's day hauling the 12.47 pm local train from Reading to Guildford between the junction of the Aldershot line and Ash station, close to the Surrey/Hampshire border. Fortunately one engine from the class, No 30120, has been preserved and can be seen in regular service, beautifully turned out in BR lined black livery, on the Mid Hants Railway, less than 20 miles from where this picture was taken. 27 January 1959. (*T B Owen*)
Leica IIIc   85mm Sonnar
Kodachrome 8   f2.3, 1/200

This picture by the same photographer as that opposite clearly shows the slight variation which existed between the last 15 members of the T9 class and the other 51, in that the former had wider cabs with full-width splashers to accommodate both driving wheels and coupling rods. Here No 30337, built at Nine Elms in 1901, is also seen on a Reading to Guildford train, this location being between Ash station and Ash Junction. Three months after the photograph was taken No 30337 was withdrawn. 20 September 1958. (*T B Owen*)
Leica IIIc   85mm Sonnar
Kodachrome 8   f2.8, 1/200

A delightful study reflecting a bygone age when train travel was very much the norm for most people, especially when taking their annual holidays. This Isle of Wight scene shows Class 02 No W35 *Freshwater* entering Brading station with the 3.42 pm Ryde Pier Head to Ventnor train during the height of the summer holiday season. Note on the up platform the enormous pile of holiday luggage waiting to be loaded on to the next train to Ryde, no doubt being sent in advance on a collection and delivery basis by homeward-bound holidaymakers. Today such civilised and convenient facilities have vanished, and if you cannot carry it yourself you simply do not take it or, worse for BR, you forget the train and load it into the family car and go off in that instead! 29 August 1964. (*Peter A Fry*)
Kodak Retinette 1B   Agfa CT18

A rare colour photograph taken at Bembridge, the most easterly station on the Isle of Wight, situated at the end of a short 2¾ mile branch from Brading (see opposite). Leaving the terminus is 02 class No W14 *Fishbourne* with two coaches in the early BR red livery then applied to non-corridor stock. This station was notable for its platform-end turntable, provided instead of the usual headshunt and turnout for an engine to run round, as space was severely restricted. This little branch was closed to all traffic in September 1953. 4 April 1953. (*J M Jarvis*)
Kodak Retina   50mm Ektar 3.5
Kodachrome 8   f4, 1/100

Below: Until the advent of the Bulleid Pacifics the 'Lord Nelsons' and 'King Arthurs' were the front line representatives of the Southern's six-coupled passenger fleet, and this picture shows the stylish appearance of the N15 class 'King Arthur' 4-6-0s. Here is No 30782 *Sir Brian*, one of the batch of 54 engines known as 'Maunsell' or 'Scotch Arthurs' because they were to Maunsell's modified design rather than the original Urie series. It was one of 30 constructed by North British Locomotive Co in 1925. *Sir Brian* is seen standing in Ashford shed yard during a sleet storm on the occasion of a commemorative 'King Arthur' class final run to the Kent Coast from Victoria organised by the LCGB. *Sir Brian* was the penultimate N15 to be withdrawn in September 1962. 25 February 1962. (*Hugh Ballantyne*)
Voigtlander CLR   50mm 2.8 Skopar

Inset: A picture taken on the same occasion as the main one below, showing the neat style of nameplate used on the 'King Arthurs' which was affixed to the continuous splasher and positioned over the centre driving wheel. All the 'Maunsell' N15s were allotted names of various Knights of the Round Table. 25 February 1962. (*Hugh Ballantyne*)
Voightlander CLR   50mm 2.8 Skopar

A striking picture taken at Ashford with a stormy sky as backcloth to No 31574, a beautiful engine showing the elegant styling of Harry Wainwright's D class 4-4-0, of which 51 were built between 1901 and 1907 for passenger work on the SECR. Twenty-one were eventually rebuilt by Maunsell as D1 class, but of the Wainwright originals this locomotive survived until 1956, the final year the class saw service. Fortunately one, No 737, is preserved in the national museum at York. August 1955. (*J M Jarvis*)

Kodak Retina   *50mm Ektar 3.5*
Kodachrome 8   *f3.5, 1/100*

On a bright autumn day a Maunsell Class S15 4-6-0 No 30833 canters down the quadruple-track LSWR main line under one of the distinctive automatic lower quadrant signal gantries near Bramshot, between Farnborough and Fleet, with the 2.54 pm Waterloo to Basingstoke train. This engine was one of a batch of 15 built at Eastleigh in 1927 and remained in traffic until May 1965. Three Maunsell S15s are preserved, two languish in the scrapyard at Barry and two of the original Urie series are also safe on the Mid Hants Railway awaiting restoration. 17 October 1964. (*Hugh Ballantyne*)
Voigtlander CLR   50mm 2.8 Skopar
Agfa CT18   f4, 1/500

Robert Urie introduced a goods 4-6-0 type in 1920 with 5 ft 7 in coupled wheels for service on the LSWR, classified S15. They had an overall resemblance to the passenger Class N15, also designed by Urie, except for their smaller coupled wheels and higher running plate over the valve gear. They were successful engines, and after the grouping Maunsell produced 25 more built in three batches between 1927 and 1936, making a class total of 45 locomotives. The Maunsell engines did not have the raised running plate and so from a distance looked even more like their passenger brothers, the N15s. Here is a very dirty No 30844, one of the last-built series, attached to a 5000 gallon flat-sided bogie tender, standing at Templecombe with the 12.16 pm three-coach local train to Salisbury, on a line where the class did much good work during their useful careers. No 30844 was withdrawn in June 1964. 27 July 1963. (*Hugh Ballantyne*)

Voigtlander CLR   50mm 2.8 Skopar
Agfa CT18   f8, 1/60

63

Left: Heading down the LSWR West of England main line into the evening sun one of the 'Eastleigh Arthurs' of N15 class, No 30455 *Sir Launcelot* comes round the curve near Pirbright Junction at the top of the long gentle rise from West Weybridge with the 6.09 pm semifast from Waterloo to Basingstoke. This engine was one of 10 ordered by Maunsell and built at Eastleigh for the Western Section of the Southern in 1925, and in common with some of the other 'Eastleigh Arthurs' spent much of its life at Salisbury shed, although when withdrawn in April 1959 its final depot was Basingstoke. 20 May 1958. (*T B Owen*)
Leica IIIc   85mm Sonnar
Kodachrome 8   f2, 1/200

Above: Class N15 No 30782 *Sir Brian*, one of the 'Scotch Arthurs', looks in good fettle here with steam to spare and well cleaned as it drifts past Bournemouth East Goods Yard box with the 4.10 pm from Southampton Terminus to Bournemouth Central local train. Behind the engine the distinctive tower of St Clement's Church can be seen. Three months after this photograph was taken *Sir Brian* was withdrawn. June 1962. (*Alan Trickett*)
Zeiss Contina   Agfa CT18

Here is a portrait of 'Merchant Navy' No 35023 *Holland Afrika Line* straddling the 50 ft diameter turntable at Templecombe Somerset & Dorset shed at a period in Southern history when there was a spate of steam specials on the Western Section and to the Somerset & Dorset line. This engine was a popular choice as motive power for main line running and on this occasion of a SCTS special the big Pacific is waiting at Templecombe to work the train back to Waterloo whilst the customers are visiting Highbridge behind class 4F No 44560. At the time this was one of nine 'Packets' allocated to Bournemouth shed, but sadly this fine engine was withdrawn in July 1967 and subsequently cut up. 28 March 1965. (*Hugh Ballantyne*)

Voigtlander CLR   50mm Skopar 2.8
Agfa CT18   f8--11, 1/60

Locomotive handling on the difficult switchback road between Salisbury and Exeter was always of the highest order, and the author well recalls how the up fast trains would sweep through Templecombe shaking the station as they galloped down to the dip in the line before the rise to Buckhorn Weston Tunnel. Those that stopped, such as this train, would come to a quick halt and as soon as possible accelerate hard out of the station so as gain maximum momentum to maintain speed for the undulating run to Salisbury. Impatient to be away, rebuilt light Pacific No 34060 *25 Squadron* pauses at Templecombe on a warm summer's day with the 8.25 am restaurant car express from Plymouth to Waterloo. 27 July 1963. (*Hugh Ballantyne*) *Voigtlander CLR   50mm Skopar 2.8 Agfa CT18   f8, 1/60*

Opposite: A scene at the terminus of Lyme Regis, one of several Southern branch lines located in East Devon and Dorset. This 6¾ mile branch, with gradients as steep as 1 in 40, was constructed under a Light Railway Order and opened in August 1903. Adams Radial 4-4-2Ts, long outliving their sisters, were successfully used on the branch from 1913 to 1961, when Ivatt 2-6-2Ts replaced them. Here Radial No 30583 is given a passing glance by one of the passengers making their way off the train and out of the station, which was inconveniently situated high above the sea on the edge of this attractive little resort. No 30583 has had a chequered career. It was built by Neilson & Co in 1885, was withdrawn in 1917 and sold, was repurchased by the Southern Railway in 1946, withdrawn a second time in July 1961 and sold again, this time to the Bluebell Railway. Circa 1960. (*D A Soggee*)
Agfa Silette
Kodachrome   f3.5, 1/125

Left: Another of the Adams Radials, No 30582, originally LSWR No 125 and built by Robert Stephenson in 1885, heading uphill towards Combpyne, the only intermediate station on the branch, with a train from Axminster to Lyme Regis. This engine amassed over two million miles during its life until withdrawal in July 1961. 2 August 1960. (*Rodney Lissenden*)
Agfa Silette   Agfa CT18

Maunsell N class Mogul No 31869 seen hard at work hauling a heavy goods train from Reading towards Guildford, near Ash. This was a regular train which produced either an N or S15 and ran in a path just behind the 9.45 am Reading to Victoria via Redhill passenger. Eighty of these very successful 5 ft 6 in Moguls were built for the SECR and Southern railways, of which 50 were assembled at Ashford from parts made at the munitions factory at Woolwich Arsenal to give employment for its staff following the Armistice, and boilers delivered from North British. One member of the class, No 31874, is preserved and is very active on the Mid Hants Railway. 21 April 1956. (*T B Owen*)

Leica IIIc   85mm Sonnar
Kodachrome 8   f2.6, 1/200

The 6 ft coupled Maunsell Moguls of U class, comprising 50 engines, were also an eminently successful design, particularly suited for the many cross-country and semi-fast services provided by the Southern. Here No 31625, built at Ashford in 1929, comes around the sharp curve at Virginia Water with a goods train off the LSWR main line at Weybridge West Junction en route to Feltham yard. Four U class engines have been preserved, including this one on the Mid Hants Railway. 23 June 1957. (T B Owen)

Leica IIIc   50mm Summitar
Kodachrome 8   f2.8, 1/100

Left: On a lovely sunny autumn day Maunsell V class 'Schools' No 30904 *Lancing* provides a magnificent sight heading eastwards on the up slow line near Winchfield with the 12.53 pm Basingstoke to Waterloo train. No 30904 was built at Eastleigh in 1930 and withdrawn in 1961. 21 November 1959. (*T B Owen*)
Leica IIIc   85mm Sonnar
Kodachrome 8   f2.3, 1/200

Above: Befitting what were at the time of building in 1926 the most powerful 4-6-0s in the country, names of British sea dogs were bestowed upon the 16 'Lord Nelsons' designed by Maunsell. Initially they did not come up to expections, but following further modifications by Bulleid after Maunsell's retirement, notably the fitting of the Lemaitre multi-blastpipe system, they became much better performers. The elegant good looks of all Maunsell designs are certainly visible in this picture of immaculate No 30863 *Lord Rodney* speeding up the main line near Bramshot with a Southampton Docks to Waterloo Boat Train special. Note the coaching stock is in the early BR passenger livery and that the sixth and seventh vehicles are Pullman cars. 6 October 1956. (*T B Owen*)
Leica IIIc   85mm Sonnar
Kodachrome 8   f2.3, 1/200

The final Southern passenger engine livery before the nationalisation of the railway in 1948 was a most attractive shade of green, described as malachite, lined yellow and black. The Isle of Wight engines were usually kept in spotless condition as clearly evidenced here, with Adams 02 class No W32 *Bonchurch* seen at Newport shed in this livery, but lettered 'British Railways' in the Southern style. This was the last Isle of Wight engine to retain malachite green, which it did until June 1953, as BR policy had decreed these engines were to be painted in the new corporate black livery. 18 May 1952. (*T B Owen*)
Leica IIIc   50mm Summitar
Kodachrome 8   f3.5, 1/60

Not quite so clean as the engine opposite but still a good livery detail picture of another LSWR 0-4-4T design, this being a Drummond M7 class, No 30241, seen in the shed yard at Nine Elms. The malachite green suited Southern engines and was extremely well set off by the lining style. By comparison there is a glimpse of the succeeding BR Brunswick green livery seen on part of the cab of 'West Country' No 34007 behind and to the left of the M7's smokebox. No 30241 was built at Nine Elms in 1899 and withdrawn in July 1963. 25 May 1952. (*T B Owen*)
Leica IIIc   50mm Summitar
Kodachrome 8   f3.5, 1/60

Left: On a rather overcast but warm summer's day, the 12.42 Waterloo to Basingstoke train hauled by U class 2-6-0 No 31624 draws out of Winchfield station with one more stop to make before reaching its destination. Except for the loss of the semaphore signals, this station has not changed greatly in modern times. For interest, readers are invited to compare this picture with that on page 39 of the publisher's companion volume 'Rail Portfolio–The 50s' by Ken Harris. 21 July 1962. *(T B Owen)*
Leica M2   50mm Summicron
Kodachrome II   f2.5, 1/250

Above: A Maunsell U class doing work to which it was well-suited, hauling a cross-country train. Here No 31618 is high up in the beautiful Cotswold Hills arriving at Withington, by then reduced to an unstaffed halt, with the only southbound train of the day on this section of the Midland & South Western Junction line, the 1.52 pm Cheltenham St James to Southampton Terminus. This former joint line was part of the Western Region which at the time appeared to be blatantly running the train service down to an abysmal level in order to successfully drive passengers away as a prelude to the inevitable

closure. This long fascinating cross-country route, once jointly owned by the two companies which gave it its name, closed in September 1961. Happily, the locomotive survives and looks superb working on the Bluebell Railway in one of the pre-war Southern green liveries. 13 May 1961. *(Hugh Ballantyne)*
Voigtlander CLR   50mm Skopar 2.8
Agfa CT18   f5.6, 1/250

77

A well known and busy location for watching the action was on the footbridges at Petts Wood Junction in Kent where the complex of lines and junctions near Bickley meet and bifurcate. Today the area of land on both sides of the train in this picture is heavily overgrown, but rebuilt 'West Country' No 34004 *Yeovil* presents a fine sight at the head of the 2.00 pm Boat Train from Victoria to Folkestone coming off the LCDR line and heading onto the SER main line towards Tonbridge and Ashford. This engine was built in 1945, rebuilt in 1958 and withdrawn at the end of Southern steam in July 1967. It had its moment of glory as it was one of three of the 'West Country' class used in the 1948 locomotive exchanges. *Yeovil* went far away to the north and worked on the Perth to Inverness line for comparative tests against an LMS Class 5 and LNER B1. The light Pacific had easily the best steam-making capacity and drawbar horsepower over its rivals, but achieved it at the expense of substantially heavier coal consumption. 4 March 1961. *(Rodney Lissenden)*
Agfa Silette   Agfa CT18

One of Maunsell's D1 class 4-4-0s, No 31739, has steam to spare on arrival at Dover Priory station with the 7.24 am (SO) train from London Bridge to Ramsgate via Tonbridge, Ashford and Dover. This train was the last regular booked working for a 4-4-0 and ceased a month after the picture was taken when the SER main line was electrified. 6 May 1961. (*Rodney Lissenden*)
Agfa Silette   Agfa CT18

79

The passage of time and familiarity have mellowed enthusiasts' feelings towards the appearance of this Bulleid wartime austerity design of 0-6-0 goods locomotive. Stark it may be, but 40 were built in 1942 with considerations of shortage of materials, route availability and weight ratio to power and size in mind, and in all aspects Bulleid was successful. They were the most powerful 0-6-0s to see service in Great Britain and did good work particularly on the Central and, until electrification, Eastern sections. Here, No 33036 stands at Guildford shed, which was always the home of half a dozen or more. Most of the class were withdrawn in 1963–64, including No 33036, but two survived until 1965 and the original engine No 33001, preserved in the national collection, is at work on the Bluebell Railway. 11 August 1963. (*Hugh Ballantyne*)
Voigtlander CLR   50mm Skopar 2.8
Agfa CT18   f8, 1/60

The attractive LBSCR station at Tunbridge Wells West seen on a wet early spring day. On the extreme left is the wall of the loco shed, now demolished, as is the building on the right, but otherwise the station remains much the same – just – as there are threats to close it. Two Bulleid engines are visible, No 34066 *Spitfire* leaving with an enthusiasts' special en route to Brighton, which it has just taken over from Q1 No 33027, visible in the bottom right of the picture. 22 March 1964. *(Hugh Ballantyne)*
Voigtlander CLR   50mm Skopar 2.8
Agfa CT18   f5.6, 1/60

Above: For reasons of geography, all the British railway companies seemed to have some important junction stations, drawing traffic from various directions, located in the most rural of surroundings and therefore not generating any originating business. This picture shows one such station, Halwill for Beaworthy, in north west Devon. It was situated on the long arm of the LSWR from Meldon Junction to Padstow. From Halwill a line went to the small north Cornish resort of Bude, and another meandered northwards over the former North Devon & Cornwall Joint Railway to Torrington and Barnstaple. During one of Halwill's daily spells of bustle this fascinating photograph shows (left to

right): BR Ivatt Class 2 2-6-2T No 41283 with the 6.30 pm to Torrington, Maunsell Mogul No 31840 pulling out with the 5.51 pm Okehampton to Wadebridge, and BR Standard Class 4 2-6-4T No 80039 with the 6.25 pm to Bude. 4 July 1964. *(Peter A Fry)*
Kodak Retinette 1B   Agfa CT18

Right: Reference has been made to the Bodmin & Wadebridge Railway on page 52 but the best known part of that railway became the goods only section from Dunmere Junction to Wenford Bridge. The reason for this was that it remained the stamping ground of three ancient

Class 0298 Beattie 2-4-0WTs which outlived the rest of the class by over 60 years. These veterans worked from Wadebridge shed and here is one of the trio, No 30587, built by Beyer Peacock in 1874, in a typical setting heading up the lovely wooded valley of the River Camel near Helland Bridge with its train of empty china clay wagons bound for Wenford Bridge. China clay was the sole reason for the existence of this branch and after the demise of the Beattie engines, two of which have been preserved, ex-GWR 1366 class 0-6-0PTs took over until dieselisation. In modern times the branch was worked by Class 08 350 hp shunters until it finally closed in 1983. June 1960. *(J M Jarvis)*

R E L Maunsell's style of locomotive design showed itself clearly throughout his career on the three railways he served as CME, the Irish Great Southern & Western, the SECR and the Southern. This big three-cylinder 2-6-4T has all his features, being based on his N1 class Moguls. Fifteen were built between 1932 and 1936 to work transfer freight services around London. By 1963 they had generally been displaced and some went to Exmouth Junction shed to bank trains up the formidable 1 in 37 incline between Exeter St Davids and Central stations. When this picture was taken of Feltham's No 31912, it was one of two survivors still in the London area and is seen in Wimbledon Down Goods Yard on a local trip working on what was one of the hottest days of the year. Within a month this engine was withdrawn. 25 July 1964. (*Hugh Ballantyne*)

Voigtlander CLR   50mm Skopar 2.8
Agfa CT18   f5.6–8, 1/60

The LSWR had a 9¾ mile long branch line traversing a peninsula forming a beautiful part of Dorset known as the Isle of Purbeck; it ran from Worgret Junction to the little seaside resort of Swanage. In a typical scene evident for many years, a Drummond M7 class 0-4-4T No 30111 stands at the main platform with an afternoon train to Wareham. Sadly the branch was closed to passenger traffic in January 1972 although the short section to Furzebrook remains for freight only. However a vigorous preservation group has saved Swanage station and is actively extending the branch inland towards Corfe Castle, location of the only intermediate station. 9 September 1962. (*G W Morrison*)
Contaflex   Tessar 2.8   Agfa CT18

Left: BR Standard classes played an important role on the Southern following their gradual introduction during the 1950s as they displaced the old pre-grouping types. In all, eight of the 12 Standard classes were allocated at some time to Southern sheds. On a lovely bright spring day Standard Class 5 No 73113 *Lyonesse* is going well up the 1 in 82 climb through the woods near Witley on the long uphill section from Godalming to Haslemere with the diverted 11.30 am Waterloo to Bournemouth train. Twenty of the Class 5s allocated to the Southern were given names previously carried by the Urie series of 'King Arthurs'. 20 March 1966. (*John Dagley-Morris*)
Kodak Retinette   Agfa CT18

Above: The Southern also received the last 15 of the Swindon-built Standard Class 4 4-6-0s. These were all fitted with double chimneys and the larger capacity BR1B tender. No 75070 spent some years at Three Bridges before moving to the South Western Division. Here it stands at Fareham on 20 March 1966 having arrived from Southampton Terminus with the RCTS 'Solent Tour', which was to be taken down the Gosport branch by a U class 2-6-0. (*Hugh Ballantyne*)
Voigtlander CLR   f2.8 Skopar
Agfa CT18   f8, 1/60

Above: Three Bridges was a junction on the main Victoria to Brighton line for branches traversing part of the lovely Weald country in Sussex to Horsham and East Grinstead. The latter branch, 6¾ miles long, became very popular with enthusiasts due to its proximity to London, beautiful setting and retention of steam traction until 1964, late on for this area, with a frequent shuttle service between the two towns. In the bay platform at Three Bridges H class 0-4-4T No 31533 is about to depart for East Grinstead and in one of the up platforms a 2-HAL electric unit is on a London-bound service. 1 April 1962. (*D A Soggee*)
Agfa Silette   Kodachrome 8   f3.5, 1/125

Right: The SER had a rural branch line of 4¾ miles from Dunton Green, on its main line to Tonbridge, to Westerham, an attractive town in north west Kent, noted as the birthplace of General Wolfe and nearest town to Chartwell, the former home of Sir Winston Churchill. The branch was worked by Wainwright H class 0-4-4Ts from Tonbridge shed, and this is a typical scene taken on a fine early autumn day, of No 31222 having just left Westerham and pushing its train of ex-railmotor coaches towards Dunton Green. The branch was closed to all traffic on 28 October 1961 and now most of the formation has been swallowed up to become a small part of the M25 London Orbital Motorway. 4 October 1959. (*Rodney Lissenden*)
Agfa Silette   Agfa CT18

Robert Urie's first design for the LSWR after he took office as CME in 1912 was a robust two-cylinder mixed traffic 4-6-0, with 6 ft coupled wheels, classified H15, the first appearing from Eastleigh Works in January 1914. The class eventually totalled 26, of which 15 appeared during Maunsell's era in 1924–25. They were mainly used on semi-fast passenger and fast goods workings over the main lines of the former LSWR, plus seaside relief trains during the summer peaks. There were slight visual differences between the Urie and Maunsell series, of which No 30476 above is one of the latter with the running plate straight, whereas the Urie engines had the running plate stepped up above the cylinders. Here No 30476, painted in the BR lined black livery applied to all the class, is leaving its home base, Eastleigh, with a local train to Portsmouth. 1961. (*Alan Trickett*)
Zeiss Contina   Agfa CT18

A portrait of 'Eastleigh Arthur' 4-6-0 No 30804 *Sir Cador of Cornwall*. This was one of the last batch of 14 built in 1926–27 for work on the Central Section and was fitted with a small six-wheel tender of 3500 gallons water capacity. Upon electrification of the Brighton line on 1 January 1933, these 'Arthurs' were transferred to the Eastern Section to assist the hard-pressed pre-grouping 4-4-0s working in Kent. Much of *Sir Cador's* time was spent allocated to either Ashford or Ramsgate depots, but again, on electrification of the Eastern Section, another and final move to the Western Section took place. Here it is seen at Eastleigh shed from where it continued to work until February 1962, the last year these handsome locomotives remained in service. 15 August 1961. (*G W Morrison*) *Contaflex*   *f2.8 Tessar*   *Agfa CT18*

As the 1960s progressed and the elimination of steam drew perceptibly nearer, standards of cleanliness declined, but paradoxically, on the Bournemouth main line services at least, enthusiastic crews drove their steeds harder and faster than ever before. Here is rebuilt 'West Country' No 34046 *Braunton* in everyday condition, quite filthy but still working hard, drawing out of Southampton Central under the magnificent signal gantry with the 1.30 pm Waterloo to Weymouth express. It is interesting to note that the 'Railway Observer' recorded in June 1967, literally during the last few weeks of steam running, that this engine had attained 95 mph on a down Bournemouth train. 30 August 1965. (*Hugh Ballantyne*)
Voigtlander CLR   50mm Skopar 2.8
Agfa CT18   f5.6, 1/250